ANNO'S MYSTERIOUS MULTIPLYING JAR

Masaichiro and Mitsumasa Anno

illustrated by Mitsumasa Anno

SCHOLASTIC INC.

New York Toronto London Auckland Sydney
Mexico City New Delhi Hong Kong Buenos Aires

This story is about one jar and what was inside it.

There was water in the jar.
It seemed as though a bit of wind was blowing
inside the jar, for the water was rippling.

The rippling water became a wide, deep sea.

On the sea was 1 island.

On the island there were 2 countries.

Within each country there were 3 mountains.

On each mountain there were 4 walled kingdoms.

Within each walled kingdom there were 5 villages.

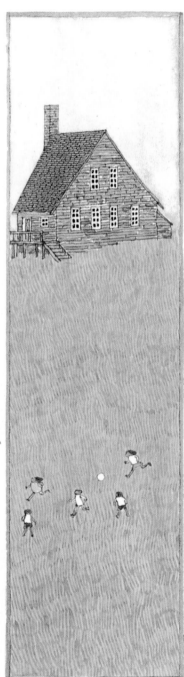

In each village there were 6 houses.

In each house there were 7 rooms.

In each room there were 8 cupboards.

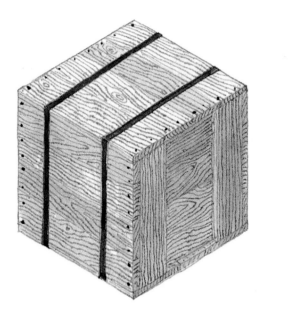

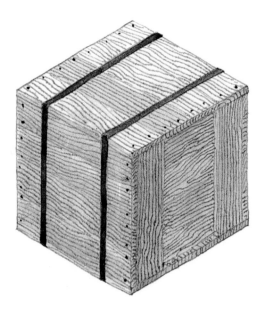

Within each cupboard there were 9 boxes.

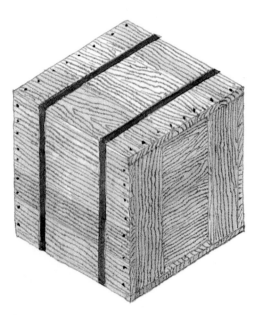

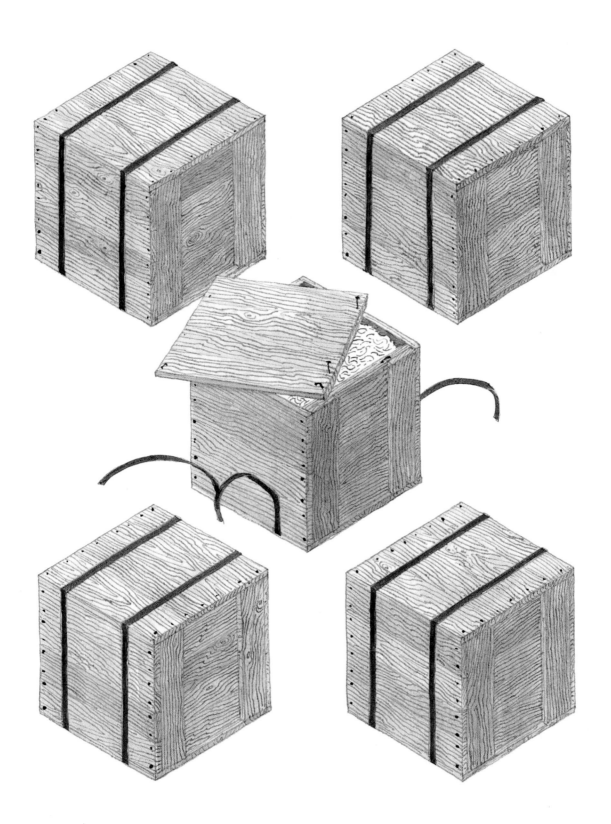

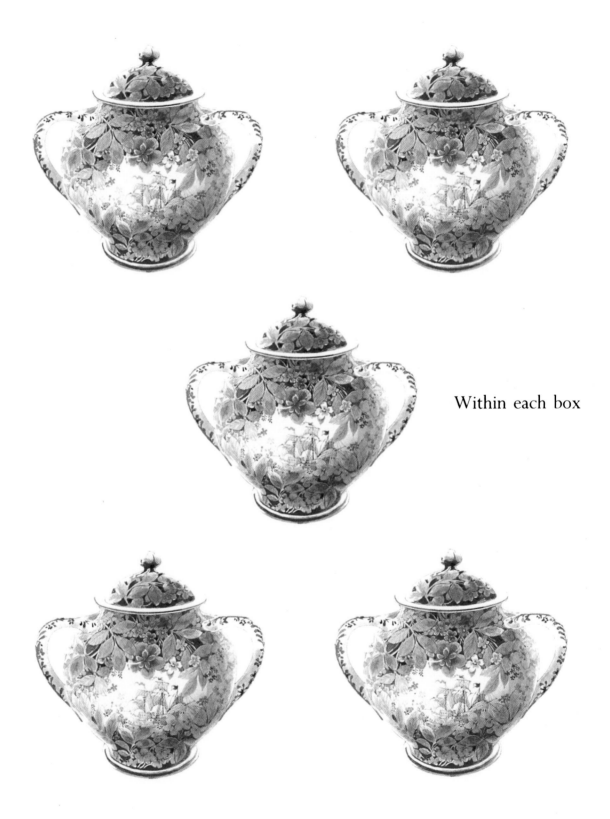

Within each box

there were 10 jars.

Within each box there were 10 jars.
But how many jars were in all the boxes together?
The answer is surprising. There were 10! jars.
But 10! does not mean just 10 jars.
10! means "10 factorial," or 3,628,800.
How did there come to be so many jars?
Let us see.

When you multiply
$10 \times 9 \times 8 \times 7 \times 6 \times 5 \times 4 \times 3 \times 2 \times 1$
you get 3,628,800. It is hard to
think about a number as big
as this. Suppose we use
dots to stand for the
things in the story:

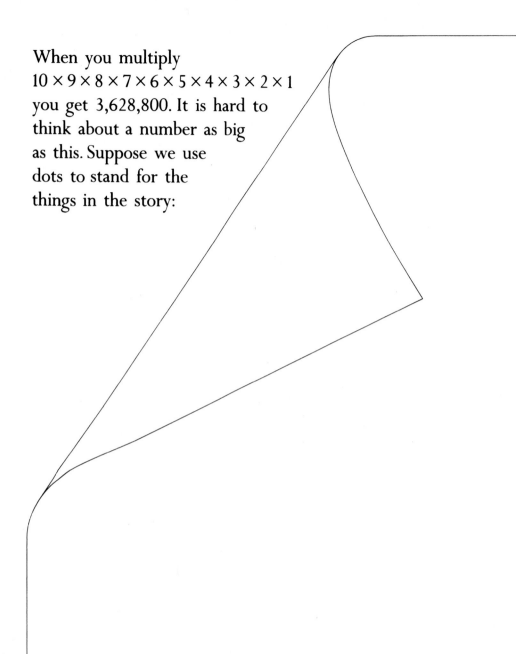

Inside the mysterious jar in the story there were some
things arranged in an ordered mathematical pattern.
First, there was water and a ship and a little imagination.
But these are not part of the pattern. The pattern
begins with the island, which is also inside the jar.

$$1! = 1 \times 1! = 1$$

On the sea was 1 island.

$$2! = 2 \times 1! = 2 \times 1 = 2$$

On the island there were 2 countries.

$$3! = 3 \times 2! = 3 \times 2 \times 1 = 6$$

⁞

Within each country there were 3 mountains.

$$4! = 4 \times 3! = 4 \times 3 \times 2 \times 1 = 24$$

On each mountain there were 4 walled kingdoms.

$$5! = 5 \times 4! = 5 \times 4 \times 3 \times 2 \times 1 = 120$$

Within each walled kingdom there were 5 villages.

$$6! = 6 \times 5! = 6 \times 5 \times 4 \times 3 \times 2 \times 1 = 720$$

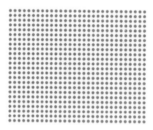

In each village there were 6 houses.

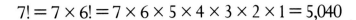

$$7! = 7 \times 6! = 7 \times 6 \times 5 \times 4 \times 3 \times 2 \times 1 = 5{,}040$$

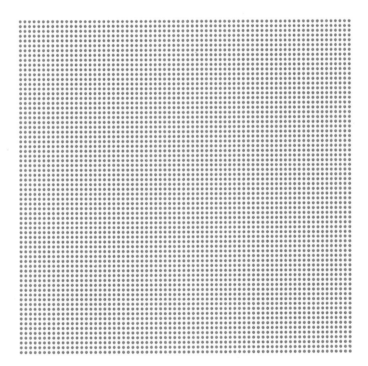

In each house there were 7 rooms.

$$8! = 8 \times 7! = 8 \times 7 \times 6 \times 5 \times 4 \times 3 \times 2 \times 1 = 40{,}320$$

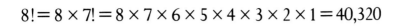

In each room there were 8 cupboards.

$$9! = 9 \times 8! = 9 \times 8 \times 7 \times 6 \times 5 \times 4 \times 3 \times 2 \times 1 = 362,880$$
$$10! = 10 \times 9! = 10 \times 9 \times 8 \times 7 \times 6 \times 5 \times 4 \times 3 \times 2 \times 1 = 3,628,800$$

Within each cupboard there were 9 boxes.

And within each box there were 10 jars.

But it took up two whole pages just to show 40,320 or $8 \times 7 \times 6 \times 5 \times 4 \times 3 \times 2 \times 1$ dots. And we still must show 9 times as many dots, or 362,880 dots, and then 10 times as many as that if we want to show how many jars there are. And to show 3,628,800 dots would take up 180 more pages in this book!

That is not a very convenient way to picture or write about large numbers. We might say that there were $10 \times 9 \times 8 \times 7 \times 6 \times 5 \times 4 \times 3 \times 2 \times 1$ dots (or jars). But that is not very easy either. Mathematicians like to find short ways to say long numbers. So a mathematician would say there are 10! or "10 factorial" jars. And he or she would know that meant 3,628,800 jars.

Afterword: A little more about Factorials

"Factorial" is a word that mathematicians use to describe a special kind of numerical relationship. The mathematical symbol for a factorial is an exclamation mark! That is the signal that the number it follows stands for the product of that number multiplied by the next smaller number, multiplied by the next smaller number, and so on all the way down to 1. An example of this is "6 factorial" which is written as 6! but which really is equal to $6 \times 5 \times 4 \times 3 \times 2 \times 1$, or 720. What would 11! mean? It is the product of $11 \times 10!$ or $11 \times 10 \times 9 \times 8 \times 7 \times 6 \times 5 \times 4 \times 3 \times 2 \times 1$ and equals 39,916,800.

Just by turning the pages of this book, you can see how quickly numbers in this kind of pattern grow—from 1 to 2 to 6 to 24 and so on to a quite stupendous number. Just seeing the simple images on the pages does not give you the impression of the whole. But if one could see it panoramically—see all the parts contained in the whole—what a surprising world would be unfolded!

Here is a list of the factorials in this story:

$$1! = 1 \times 1! = 1 = 1 \text{ (island)}$$
$$2! = 2 \times 1! = 1 \times 2 = 2 \text{ (countries)}$$
$$3! = 3 \times 2! = 1 \times 2 \times 3 = 6 \text{ (mountains)}$$
$$4! = 4 \times 3! = 1 \times 2 \times 3 \times 4 = 24 \text{ (walled kingdoms)}$$
$$5! = 5 \times 4! = 1 \times 2 \times 3 \times 4 \times 5 = 120 \text{ (villages)}$$
$$6! = 6 \times 5! = 1 \times 2 \times 3 \times 4 \times 5 \times 6 = 720 \text{ (houses)}$$
$$7! = 7 \times 6! = 1 \times 2 \times 3 \times 4 \times 5 \times 6 \times 7 = 5{,}040 \text{ (rooms)}$$
$$8! = 8 \times 7! = 1 \times 2 \times 3 \times 4 \times 5 \times 6 \times 7 \times 8 = 40{,}320 \text{ (cupboards)}$$
$$9! = 9 \times 8! = 1 \times 2 \times 3 \times 4 \times 5 \times 6 \times 7 \times 8 \times 9 = 362{,}880 \text{ (boxes)}$$
$$10! = 10 \times 9! = 1 \times 2 \times 3 \times 4 \times 5 \times 6 \times 7 \times 8 \times 9 \times 10 = 3{,}628{,}800 \text{ (jars)}$$

Many things or events occur in this same kind of numerical pattern. When you know this, you can use factorials to tell you some amusing or useful things. *Anno's Mysterious Jar* is a story. But you can apply the device that runs through this book to other circumstances.

Let's say that there are 5 persons named A, B, C, D, and E who have to arrange their desks in a schoolroom. There is no special seating order. Now, how many ways are there to arrange the desks? With only 1 student at 1 desk, there is only one possibility: A. But as soon as there are 2 students and 2 desks, there are two ways they could be seated: A B or B A. Now when C comes along with another desk, there are six different ways they could be arranged: C A B , A B C , A C B , C B A , B A C, B C A. And here is how 4 persons can arrange their 4 desks:

A B C D,	A B D C,	A D B C,	D A B C,
A C B D,	A C D B,	A D C B,	D A C B,
C A B D,	C A D B,	C D A B,	D C A B,
B A C D,	B A D C,	B D A C,	D B A C,
B C A D,	B C D A,	B D C A,	D B C A,
C B A D,	C B D A,	C D B A,	D C B A.

Now you can begin to see the pattern of these possible arrangements. The number of possibilities can be expressed as factorials. When there were 4 students and 4 desks, the number of possible different seating arrangements was 4! or $4 \times 3 \times 2 \times 1$, or 24.

And the number of possible different arrangements for 5 students with 5 desks would be 5! or 120. For 10 students with 10 desks there would be 10! possibilities, and you know how big a number that is. How many different seating arrangements are possible in your classroom?

Once you start noticing these patterns of numbers, you can make very good guesses about things like your chances of being on the same team as your best friend, or of being seated next to him or her at a party.

$$
\begin{aligned}
11! &= 11 \times 10! = & 39{,}916{,}800 \\
12! &= 12 \times 11! = & 479{,}001{,}600 \\
13! &= 13 \times 12! = & 6{,}227{,}020{,}800 \\
14! &= 14 \times 13! = & 87{,}178{,}291{,}200 \\
15! &= 15 \times 14! = & 1{,}307{,}674{,}368{,}000 \\
16! &= 16 \times 15! = & 20{,}922{,}789{,}888{,}000 \\
17! &= 17 \times 16! = & 355{,}687{,}428{,}096{,}000 \\
18! &= 18 \times 17! = & 6{,}402{,}373{,}705{,}728{,}000 \\
19! &= 19 \times 18! = & 121{,}645{,}100{,}408{,}832{,}000 \\
20! &= 20 \times 19! = & 2{,}432{,}902{,}008{,}176{,}640{,}000
\end{aligned}
$$

Learning about numbers and how they can expand almost without limit by such simple means as are shown in this book will, we hope, give readers an idea of the remarkable order that underlies our universe, and a sense of the mystery, wonder, and excitement that can be experienced through mathematics.

Masaichiro and Mitsumasa Anno

About Mitsumasa Anno

Mitsumasa Anno was born in 1926 in Tsuwano, a small historic town in the western part of Japan. He graduated from Yamaguchi Teacher Training College and then worked as a primary-school teacher before starting his career as an artist. Mr. Anno now lives in Tokyo, but he is a regular traveler to Europe and has also visited the United States. His books are beloved by children (and their parents) the world over.

About Masaichiro Anno

Masaichiro Anno is the son of Mitsumasa Anno and shares his father's enthusiasm for art, science and mathematics. He was born in Tokyo in 1954, graduated from the School of Science and Engineering of Waseda University in Tokyo, and is now working in advertising. He and his father have previously collaborated on *Anno's Magical ABC: An Anamorphic Alphabet.*

Original Japanese edition published in 1982 by Dowaya, Tokyo, as *Tsubo No Naka*.

ISBN 978-0-439-84776-6

7 8 9 10   40   15 16 17 18/0